Praise for Heather Lang-Cassera

Firefall is a deftly crafted lyrical meditation on the relationship between environment, the body, and the ways in which each inhabits the other. In this collection, the landscape wears our bruises, fills with our ghosts, and invites us to look inward, compare the damage. Through this lens, each poem's use of sound and repetition reminds the reader how abundant the world within and around us is, was, and could be if only we'd look at it with the right kind of attention. A quiet, necessary journey with a clear and urgent call: "do not underestimate the traces/ we have swiftly/ made of us." Lang-Cassera's writing is as powerful as it is captivating.

> —Samuel Piccone, author of *Pupa* (Anhinga Press, 2017), Editor's Choice in the 2017 Rick Campbell Chapbook Prize

Once in a great while, a book comes along that alters you in ways you cannot describe. You know only that something within you has shifted, the landscape that was is no longer, and you must begin again. Heather Lang-Cassera's *Firefall* will bring you to this place—to a world "stark and untamed," a place both ferocious and quiet where you will need to simultaneously reach down into the earth while bringing "the sky into the palms of [your] hands." These poems will follow you into the garden you had only allowed yourself to hope for and onto the trail you thought you knew by memory. They will stand with you on the shore when the storm approaches. They will ignite a fire within you that inspires you to begin your own quiet revolution. This is "the call of the canyon wren [descending]," the place where the "anchored nail meets the moon," your personal call to action. These poems are essential reading and will leave their mark in the best possible way.

—Letisia Cruz, author of *Migrations & Other Exiles* (Lost Horse Press, 2023), winner of the 2022 Idaho Prize for Poetry

Firefall

Heather Lang-Cassera

UNSOLICITED
PRESS
PORTLAND, OREGON
SINCE 2012

Through a Project Grant for Artists, the writing of this book was supported in part by the Nevada Arts Council and the National Endowment for the Arts.

For information contact:

Unsolicited Press

Portland, Oregon

www.unsolicitedpress.com

orders@unsolicitedpress.com

619-354-8005

Cover Design: Kathryn Gerhardt

Editor: Summer Stewart

ISBN: 978-1-963115-23-9

Versions of some of these poems first appeared in Barnstorm Journal, Black Fox Literary Magazine, Bryant Literary Review, Clark County Public Arts' Group Text exhibition, Desert Companion's Fifth Street by Nevada Public Radio, Devoid Magazine, the Double Down Blog by Nevada Humanities, Heavy Feather Review, The Hopper, Interim, Modern Poetry Review, Number S#gns Poetry Project, Poetry of the Wildflowers (Tiny Seed Press), Raleigh Review, and Where Hunger Must Be Feral (rinky dink press).

Firefall

Waking to an ocean on fire where morning's first light
graces a cheekbone like an aerial perch for every song
we have unsung, follows constellations urgent as blooms
of delicate wildflowers, meadows made of never-ending
shadows, temperate belongings, absent coasts—
we witness our collective breath as wings pinned to maps
by gravity, by longing, by quickened stars, here
where affection has been hidden in
the voiceless whispers found in the ferocity
of coordinates

    stark and untamed.

Upon knowing swan song as myth,
this shelter, for a moment—

what shame was grown
into what thicket, what grief,
what breath brushed clear

to the exclusion of any other,
surrounded once more,

abandonment saying everything

without these tangled verses
performed mouth by mouth,

enmeshed misunderstandings,
bridges too merciful
to be permanent.

The unlit rockslide, this silent geography—

how we can see wind through sediment
and light, yet cannot know

how jawbone itself
might be guttural.

Bell's vireos bloom like staccato thought
clouds, and they ask us if, now, we are caught
between spring and summer beneath the light
of the only sun we can know. When might
we become breathless or merely voiceless
or needing of more than our want. Say *yes*
to the choral-throated canyons, quiet
only in expectation. Unquiet
arches like sunrise behind Keystone Thrust,
moonrise, by always city lights, hushed.
Gathering water at the root, like warm
hands map the birdcage of the heart, the storm
waits beyond the wash, where olive-gray wings
chatter, and this chamber of sandstone sings.

The news carries like a coyote
howling away

from the scruff
of her lover. Bristlecones
sip the moon-water, long

toothed and rustling
like a hiker, lost,
                tracing steps
never taken, blushing beneath

near-winter. Ponds of light
            shiver like hunger,
shadows of fur
and spine forgotten, nothing
the same. Together, through

these parched riverbeds,
we search and we
sing,
        breathless.

This ravine yawns more slowly than we can
tell time, mountain-toothed and ready for this
moment, a reminder that a wingspan
will stretch beyond this water-laced abyss,
a bit like holding one's breath, quiet in
love. The call of the canyon wren descends,
bright-throated and eloquent. We begin
again. Granite narrows make amends
with this desert sky, which has dimmed its light
and traces dry rock faces we will never
understand. The silver cholla, polite,
reflects stoic in the silence however
loud its touch might be. There is something here,
amidst empty hands, gorgeous and austere.

Waiting for the unbeloved sheep
after dusk, we forget

this raucous light is where
anchored nail meets the moon.

After dusk, we forget
the wrist that holds the hammer, while

anchored nail meets the moon,
taps out rhythms of the heart.

The wrist that holds the hammer, while
this flickering question

taps out rhythms of the heart,
gathers a brief crown of flowers.

A flickering question,
in the impulsive, quickening water,

gathers a brief crown of flowers
waiting for the unbeloved sheep.

Delicate enough to be risked,
always empty
by running, pink & bleating
with wilderness,

new homes choose
the undeniable, the forest, frenetic,
the cobalt morning. You touch them

apart from me, an unnerving
room, unidentifiable. My name
watches me.

I walk the length
of the floorboard rivers, my hand's
shadow apprehensive but
ready, silent as a sliver of sharp

paper. The possible, the darkness,
the huddled dirty at the hem,

the woodland smoke scratches
at the door, like a compass bloomed

& broken, a safety pin
no longer blanketed by wildflower
corsage, a place that
is anywhere but here—

a flock of birds, tissue thin
from where we stand,

a life, an object exposed, yet unspoiled,
mistaken & unchangeable, like someone
in grey wool socks, drenched,
coming back, to you, before winter.

The night sky wrings itself out
until becoming nothing.

We only wait
    grinding teeth like stars
into everything.

To the north   the sparrow
has slipped his tune
from three notes
to two—surely somewhere

there must be a breath.
    Without muscle memory
we only turn our backs

arms   steady
antlers   in the moonlight.

This dream is not wingbeat, nor gunshot, nor
  ancestor salvaged from this splintered oar.
Near the rust-veiled moon, remembrances wait,
  deep breath before sonic boom, silent gate
tapping its foot in the wind like a still
  grave—a lava tube midnight light will fill.
We ask too many questions: who, and where?
  None of them are right. Burroweed and spare
nowheres, dust glossy through these thick windows,
  this desert is a woodwind, its shadows
ready for mistakes. Stark basin washes—
  these riverbeds like a spine that flinches,
a vessel that holds water at its most
  vulnerable, gritting its teeth, a ghost.

This A-frame in flames,
      a prayer collapsed again.
This smoke, hushed murmur

      unheard, yet seen, not salvaged—
      this fire started from inside.

Sheets of frost-gathered lace
trim the slender window

by which you sleep
every night.

Trim the slender window
with gifts from the exquisite ghosts.

Every night,
the mundane stars sway

with gifts from the exquisite. Ghosts
then fade into the heart, leave behind

the mundane. Stars sway
with us in sotto voce,

then fade. Into the heart, leave behind
the bedframe for these rooftop trusses.

With us, in sotto voce—
Sheets of frost? Gathered lace.

Found

     beneath the snow,
we leave our words, flowers

     amongst strangers.

Every theatre has a ghost.

You were the one to cut
the illusionist himself in half
with your followspot;
to light him at low level;

to hold the cable with perfect
tension in the dark, before the shift
in zenith, and then coil

quickly hand over hand;

to walk past mirrors,
O, such sweet tacenda,
meant to make it seem
as if no one were there;

to witness the showman
parade around the passerelle

on stoic stallion as stark
white as the lies we now tell

ourselves. Yet, amongst tigers
with names like Mirage,
who could remember
that horse that appeared
only once per show,

but whose hooves shattered

the lights within
that palatial stage each night.
You were the one who fixed them.

When you returned home after midnight
smelling like Montecore or Cashmere,
your house cat would hiss,

demand you cry peccavi,
and then rub her face against

your penumbral-black denim
telling you where you belonged.

What did she sense in herself
in the ingravescent afterthought
of those beautiful beasts—

was it magic, ossified, too familiar?

When need is not enough,
       dovetails lift
from the kitchen floor
       where perfect angles of tile
wait beyond this cusp of night.
       From the kitchen floor,
slender feet become porcelain.
       Wait. Beyond this cusp of night,
we cannot run with these
       slender feet. Become porcelain,
O heart, in this delicate winter.
       We cannot run with these
snow-topped silhouettes,
       O heart. In this delicate winter,
wrists have tangled together—
       snow-topped silhouettes,
dovetails, lift.

We bring the sky into the palms of our hands,
in a way, even if only a small piece.
When we embrace a lover,
holding them means only a part of them.

In a way, even if only a small piece,
this ascent of jawbone,
holding them, means only a part of them
can feign safety in the aftermath of the earthquake.

This ascent of jawbone
brings us to our toes, starward. We
can feign safety. In the aftermath of the earthquake,
recollection of the moth, who barely drinks,

brings us to our toes. Starward, we
rest where your dog killed the rabbit, a sunrise
recollection. Of the moth, who barely drinks,
her mouth is nothing like the cusps of teeth.

Rest. Where your dog killed the rabbit, sunrise
quiets the Canis Minor constellation.

Her mouth is nothing like the cusps of teeth
we see, is sometimes what we want. The belief

quiets. The Canis Minor constellation
predicts the salt heliotrope. For now, nothing
we see is sometimes what we want, the belief.
We leave alone all that this unbloomed scorpion flower

predicts. The salt heliotrope, for now nothing
we know to admire, will feed Gambel's quails, slow in flight.
We leave alone. All that this unbloomed scorpion flower
might uncoil can soothe through these punctures.

We know to admire will. Feed Gambel's quails. Slow in flight,
we can still run quickly. We
might uncoil, can soothe. Through these punctures,
we bring the sky, into the palms, of our hands.

Bees ghost line
    the shadows, moonburst
in reverse.

Please, tell me
the story   one more time?

Again, we steep ourselves
in reflection,
burn toast & eat

marmalade   near midnight.

Sometimes pity invites hyacinths
reckless in our misunderstanding.

Near the hidden water, good
things follow, softly, the torrential night.
Paradigm skies, hellos, goodbyes,
tap at the precipice of density,

of petal, of indirect light, of

dead-end's yawning, demands merely
recommended by experts
in neither fight

nor flight, spilled
beneath the sun's nearly
noontime height

as this bouquet of clouds
& their shadows.

A creosote explodes in slow motion,
blooms like a supernova, something

we witness through science, something chosen

by the beholder, unavoidable
impulse, shallow taproots interwoven

again and again. We all need water,

bones formed like dripstone, like quick erosion,
like knowing and not knowing, becoming

an ever-arid cloud, each past unchosen.

The other porch,
    the heroic rhetoric,
the choir, the chirp, the riot

& the echo   cipher ochre,
perch to home
    the petrichor.

Where you are, it is tomorrow.
A mercy
        of bristlecone trembles
in its reticence—

we are learning to disrupt our own barriers,
not looking toward where
we want to go.

The tires' ribs leave silent
prints on these parched feet

& these folded ankles have little
        to do with god; it is good
to know the sibilance of this slender pain.

The meek wind which gathers

the feral lavender, leans
        within itself—

do not underestimate the traces
        we have swiftly
made of us.

A sprig

of parsley clings
       to a pattern of metal bars—

a capsized
grocery cart.

Not wanting to care
for the pigeons, such small wanderers,
their patterns of negative night sky bodies,

not wanting to love
their heart-curved flesh,
too large for the dry riverbeds
of my hands,

not wanting to justify my unshadowed
tenderness for something
buoyed and overripe and understanding
of her own need,
and surrounded by silent songbirds,

not wanting two wings almost identical
in symmetry, shadows
that smother the ground,

not wanting invisible tongues
of perfect pink oleander
forever pressing onward
even in this arid sky—

a birth cry, a death breathing, an intangible
sun, a heap of inconsolable hope
available only from yesterdays,

these fingers become bandages
for everything
in my body that might someday be broken,

the obscurity of other blunt souls
dredges bee pollen
as bright sorrow,

horizons as weeping everything,
murmurs as fragile bundles,

anguish illuminated
in each of these
exquisite gallopings.

The ghost light—

the nightlight keeps its sloping hum,
      an invisible sound.
A home exhales, *line*,
      rests in a dark theatre.

An invisible sound
      like empty spoon, like brimming fear,
rests in a dark theatre,
      curtains made of pink carnations.

Like empty spoon, like brimming fear,
      the storms came before morning,
curtains made of pink carnations
      tossing petals in the cold rain.

The storms came. Before morning,
      the wood was riverscape, the bicycle still.
Tossing petals, in the cold rain,
      the nightlight keeps its sloping hum.

The song waits, stoic
in the rain, broken-beaked, ready
for this

       tomorrow.

The land is feral.

I've known the winter sky,
a feathered creature,

the wilderness wrapped around it.
The night is not
as dark as we make it.

It waits for us, tundra-footed and tender.

Perhaps we could witness the sound
of sandalwood
like a birth-year resting against
cage beneath collarbone,

the fog like a mane
brushing, by happenstance,
against one's own cheek.

Beyond the whimper of fire,
I will call for you,

this viscous memory walking barefoot in this
fragile morning.

Hunger lives within
the creases of my hands, never
quite knowing the patience
of need.

The memories I have forgotten,
the dorsal fins of freshwater fish,
long ago became the silver

of rafters above a home
ever in invocation, and then
never again.

In this modest light, I don't need to be everywhere,
like a metronome,
a rhythm, the firefly starlight,
like toothmarks left again.

These dark mountains might
sing meteorite,

space rock,

from foil-tight
sky, a hum

goodnight, small talk

trying to make
right this vast
city   gridlock.

Vector love waits for us, simmers in this
noon light, predictable but to someone
else. The equator will rise, reminisce
over never-failed youth, the sun homespun

and quiet in each way but that which might
matter. The crack of a wooden baseball
bat may never leave the trace of first-light
cut grass, sidewalks rerouted, cities sprawled.

Here, at times, dogs walk themselves.
Sheet metal growling in the Mojave
wind, styrofoam homes, still empty bookshelves,
and newly found cats, these howling bodies,

surround the church bells. There is no waiting.
Our hands, as fences, dampen hearts, permitting.

The number 10 (x.) is a window of multitudes, ecosystem of decimal, lung collapsed and re-opened. If close enough, even a speck of dust would eclipse the moon. A breath, pressed, as purple-mountain petals, exhales in all directions. These once-broken bones are now stunted coral, a static code as staccato as the sting of unworried sea nettle. Before scales hollow the sunlight, mouths burst into sacrament. Vertebrae turn into honeycomb. The low sky of a lost alphabet, your heart sketches its own diagram for every missed opportunity. Love is a fetal memory for what we cannot understand, kept cradled in the curl of each of our empty fingers, every unit of sound. Only this I know for certain—morning will be the wildfire at the foot of our bed. We cannot be the radial symmetry of the starfish, nor of fruit, nor of fossil.

Alluvial by maker,
this bare-shouldered allure, in a place
where meander means path, not action

to be taken, this
automatic drawing, ready & readymade,

is scalebroom, sugarbush, riparian woodland,

this small-statured
woollystar & slender-horned
spineflower, now

on private land, often
unprotected.

Tell the story of stillness,
a nearness, in the stranger
who waits for you beyond roads,

a careful unknown. Name her.

Dry-mouthed rivers, unobscured,
have not lured us to the brink

of an untamable
past, species fastened, soft
pink latched.

Unwitnessed memories,
a pangea of fricative sounds,

are dampened to reticence
by dark agave light. Some days the hunger
of not knowing

is a breath taken
from the nooks

of lungs, a need
not met, a halo of cholla
feigning tenderness.

Rain falls, and petrichor greets
us.

The streets fill with children,
a time-lapse   of constellations in early
day,
            which are quickly hidden.

The nest, the lint, the
fire which could have happened,

the oleander opening
white-hot petals in the Mojave summer
of our back yards
amidst our failing
houses,

the faceless triceratops
figurine, capsized on the sidewalk,
reminding us of an article about climate
change, one about how, just maybe,
global warming also brought about
the dinosaurs, yet we have neither
feather nor scale despite
weathered faces
from too many days of sun,

and this too shall pass,
the clouds and their quivering bodies,

because even something made
of so much water
can be considered as such,

an impulse to compare the momentary cracks
of lightning
to the fractured pavement
on which we walk, our feet
skipping like heartbeats
in chests deep and scared of thunder,
a burst of sound echoing, saying what
we never quite could,

while the fragments of unfound
solitude sift
through the corrugation
of a new-refrigerator box, emptied
and abandoned,
amidst the soft, light
wood-like, but not quite, smell
of cardboard
waiting carefully just beyond the curb,

with all this
tender kindling our mouths
cannot preserve.

Alone I wait for the ocotillo,
        reds that can only mean desert summer,

and the metallic smell of my car feels
        something like Sunday mornings—our father's

suburban when parked in a place where we
        did not live long enough, where some of our

strongest memories are of us as sheep
        leaping over Dad and one another

while he napped on the carpeted floor,
        phone cord wrapped around the couch and sweeter

dreams. I could not imagine a dim shore,
        a home larger than a house, where water

waits for us to save ourselves. Near this lake,
        the coyotes howl while the leaflets shake.

The unrequited look
to tomorrow, feather
and wind in the unexpected.
You already have your own
marrow, bone and brilliance,
your ribcage and respite.
We are not to decide
lock-stepped meanings
of anything sky-written
and beginning to disappear,
unkept, already so we cannot
understand. We trace small,
wing-shaped silhouettes
before moonset, shadow
puppets of the sycamore.

A touch of illumination   in the cave—

an olm, a swiftlet,

a decade of hunger   bristle
mouthed in absolute

darkness. Stolen nests
and everything

that cannot be carried   capture

a space that holds secrets, sifts
an entirety.
The water strikes

the light away from which they move.

Near salted walls, land lipped and slope bellied,

the crested cliff becomes
a brink   now just out of reach.

Everything waits,
     and we must be still
to find it. Rhyolite shivers
in the morning,

theatrical in its unintention,
harbinger of the quiet.

Endangered
the sun will rose-quartz
      the sky   as lizard tracks barbwire
their way   throughout
      the yellow desert   daisies.

Tonight   broken-glass
memories make night-new constellations
as siblings
      like fallen pinecones   gesture
toward everyone   but themselves.

Are these   clouds
what love might become—
      disappearing   bighorn sheep
that whisper
      with everything   that has
been
      undone?

Near Ash Spring—
we bundle memories like galaxy,
hoping that if we name them, gravity
will become nothing more than a label.
Pushing cloud-ward, palms open, the stable
door closes with a metallic click, bright
like what runs through our veins, curved and so light
that tomorrow's permanence will breed for
us atmosphere. Here, and now, is one more
breath-like bloom of sun veiled in our upturned
encore of mesa-laced mistakes. Concerned,
even heart-red sandstone blushes our cheeks,
your hand tracing your collarbone, these peeks,
these clearings, these basins. Your feet, arched,
sing of joy, of grief, of friction, parched.

Your voice is a comet
     electric. Do not wait

in this terrestrial aquarium
     of slumber. Number us

electric. Do not wait.
     Staccato wisps of thought are not

of slumber. Number us
     & these gently wasted days.

Staccato wisps of thought are not
     echoes of a small fawn song—

& these? Gently wasted. Days
     ask us to be in revolution.

Echoes of a small fawn song,
     this shudder of forest understory,

ask us to be. In revolution,
     your voice is a comet.

The oleanders are in bloom
like much

of the year. At noon we look
to one another for answers—

through plans, through

action, through shadows
uncreased.

Bones of bedrock go on
like vitrified lace,
spoon over spoon never quite
the same, saved in a place where
the heat taps the ground
like a broken egg or a new
beginning just after
each morning
staggered, emptied, somehow released.

Wanting water, here is where I return
        to when I am feeling without you,
when object permanence

fails me, when the ocean perch
        within my chest turns
into a ruby-throated hummingbird

and then back
        into a fish out of water yet again
all without ever being seen.

But, in the end, everything
        is hidden from at least somebody.
It is pisces season. What we let go

can be written down and then burned
        and then, instead of buried, lost
within the moon water

which was made by abandoning
        open-mouthed vessels beneath
this late-night light.

This time, under this
    terrestrial body, it can only
be the small things that we let go.

When we were young,
    you would look up asking
to be held.

Would our mother empty
    her vacant pockets, pulling
them inside out

as if ebbing like tidal flow,
    as if each denim basin could be
an entire sea, only

to say no, to say she had nothing
    more to offer. What does it mean
that I am so much older

than you were when you died.
    Why can I no longer
remember the shape

of you, sister, when
     you would
swim.

Index of First Lines (in order of appearance)

About the Author

Heather Lang-Cassera is an author and ceramist. She was awarded a 2022 Nevada Arts Council Literary Arts Fellowship, served as the 2019-2021 Clark County, Nevada Poet Laureate, and was named 2017 Best Local Writer or Poet by the readers of Nevada Public Radio's *Desert Companion*. Heather teaches creative writing with Nevada State University where she serves as a faculty advisor for *300 Days of Sun*. She also serves as the Poetry Editor for *Black Fox Literary Magazine*, as an Editor with Tolsun Books, and as an Instructor with Clay Arts Vegas. Her previous collection, *Gathering Broken Light* (Unsolicited Press, 2021), was written with the support of a Nevada Arts Council Project Grant for Artists, was named a Distinguished Favorite by the Independent Press Awards, and won the NYC Big Book Award in Poetry, Social/Political. She is also the author of the micro-collection *Where Hunger Must Be Feral* (rinky dink press, 2024) and the chapbook *I was the girl with the moon-shaped face* (Zeitgeist Press, 2018).

About the Press

Unsolicited Press is based out of Portland, Oregon and focuses on the works of the unsung and underrepresented. As a womxn-owned, all-volunteer small publisher that doesn't worry about profits as much as championing exceptional literature, we have the privilege of partnering with authors skirting the fringes of the lit world. We've worked with emerging and award-winning authors such as Shann Ray, Amy Shimshon-Santo, Brook Bhagat, Kris Amos, and John W. Bateman.

Learn more at unsolicitedpress.com. Find us on twitter and instagram.

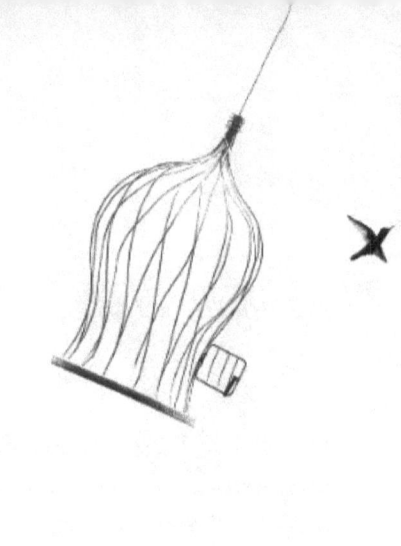

www.ingramcontent.com/pod-product-compliance
Lightning Source LLC
Chambersburg PA
CBHW031254120626
46545CB00007B/2814